Letterland

Far Beyond ABC

T0347180

Written by Lisa Holt & Lyn Wendon
Original illustrations by Doreen Shaw & Geri Livingston
Adapted by Isabelle Nicolle & Laura Bittles
Based on characters originated by Lyn Wendon.

Read to me!

This book includes FREE **'Read to me'** audio. Scan the QR code
with your mobile or tablet to start listening! Find out more at:
www.letterland.com/read-to-me

About Letterland

Letterland is an imaginary place where letters come to life! The friendly Letterland characters help children to easily understand the sound and shape of letters – one of the key skills needed when learning to read and write.

Simple stories about the Letterland characters explain letter sounds and shapes, so that confusion over similar looking letters is avoided and children are motivated to listen, think and learn.

One of Letterland's keys to success is its 'Sound Trick'. By just starting to pronounce a character's name, such as 'a...' (Annie Apple), 'b...' (Bouncy Ben), 'c...' (Clever Cat), a child automatically says the correct letter sound. It's that simple! The combination of memorable characters and proven educational principles makes Letterland the ideal way to introduce your child to the alphabet. Moving on from the alphabet, presented in the *Letterland ABC Book*, Letterland teaches all 44 letter sounds in the English language through stories rather than rules. The stories explain the sounds letters make when they come together in words. Learning new spelling patterns is wonderfully child-friendly with Letterland! You will find many of these stories in *Beyond ABC* and all the rest in this *Far Beyond ABC Book*.

For more information, including a pronunciation guide for all the letter sounds, see: www.letterland.com

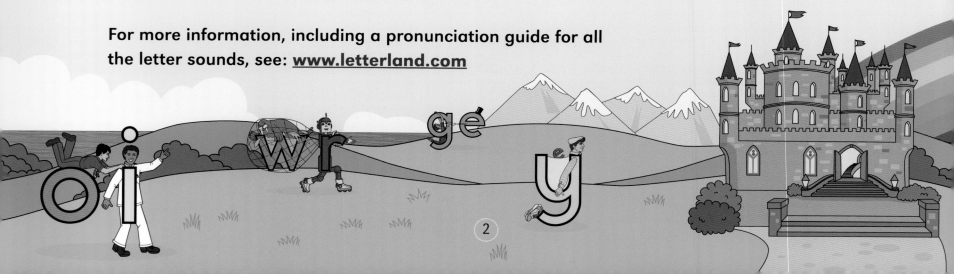

About This Book

This *Far Beyond ABC Book* is the sequel to the *Beyond ABC Book* (revised edition). It transports young readers to the imaginary world of Letterland where letters spring to life and their sounds are taught in a unique story format. These brief, beautifully-illustrated stories give child-friendly reasons why, when certain letters come together, they make a completely new sound.

Whether at home or school, children quickly discover how easy it is to remember spelling patterns by learning the stories. They'll also enjoy checking the Word List at the back of the book with your help to see if they have spotted all the objects in each scene.

The Letterland approach to teaching reading has been popular for over 50 years and meets research-based guidelines for teaching phonics. Best of all, each story is like a magic key to learning. It unlocks the new sound and makes it easy for children to read lots of other similar words - even if they've never seen them before!

Welcome back to Letterland

You probably already know that the people and animals in Letterland usually hide behind their plain black letter shapes. In this book you can look into their secret land again and discover some more Letterland stories about what happens when these characters come together in words.

Are you ready?
Let's go!

Watch out when there's a robot about. They usually cause trouble in words! Sometimes they steal letters so you can't hear them. Or if there is a vowel behind a robot's back, don't expect that vowel to be making its usual sound. It will be too startled to speak!

The Vowel Stealing Robots will try to stop you from reading the words! The best way to stop them is to become a detective! Whenever you see a robot with one vowel behind his back, don't let him trick you into saying the vowel's usual sound. Instead catch him out by calling out that robber's last name:
Arthur **Ar**, Orvil **Or**, Ernest **Er**, Irving **Ir** or Urgent **Ur**!

Sometimes the robots are so daring they even capture Vowel Men while they are out walking together. Then you won't hear the Vowel Men talking at all. You'll hear the robot shouting out instead!

Let's meet some of these robots and learn their naughty tricks!

In Letterland, there are five roller-skating robots who cause trouble by capturing vowels even though they know they shouldn't. This one is called **Ar**thur **Ar** and he likes to capture Letterland apples. Look! He is running away with Annie Apple! She is too surprised to make her usual sound. Instead, all you can hear is **Ar**thur **Ar** reporting back to the ringleader, Red Robot, with his last name, "**Ar!**"

Arthur **Ar** waited until it was getting d**ar**k. He thought he could get up to his tricks by the light of the st**ar**s, but now he's stuck trying to escape from a l**ar**ge b**ar**n! The gu**ar**d dog has st**ar**ted b**ar**king to raise the al**ar**m. And now the f**ar**mer has found **Ar**thur's rad**ar** c**ar** p**ar**ked in his y**ar**d. **Ar**thur **Ar** is d**ar**ting around the b**ar**n trying to escape, but there's a guit**ar**, and t**ar**ts, sh**ar**p d**ar**ts and j**ar**s of v**ar**nish in his way. Even a little **ar**madillo is trying h**ar**d to catch **Ar**thur **Ar** and stop him from getting away in his rad**ar** c**ar**!

c**ar**   f**ar**mer   g**ar**den   st**ar**

Now you need to learn about **Or**vil **Or**. He's another robot in Letterland who causes trouble by capturing vowels! **Or**vil **Or** likes to run away with oranges. When he is around, don't expect Oscar Orange to make his usual sound. All you can hear is **Or**vil **Or** rep**or**ting back to Red Robot with just one word, his last name, '**Or**!' as he rushes away to his boat by the sh**or**e.

Can you see **Or**vil's boat by the sh**or**e? It looks very st**or**my over there, doesn't it? There's an en**or**mous t**or**nado coming. It's heading for the **or**chard so unf**or**tunately the children playing sp**or**ts will have to run ind**oor**s. The st**or**m hasn't stopped **Or**vil **Or** though. As he f**or**ces his way past the h**or**se, it gives a little sn**or**t. But he had better not step on that little p**or**cupine. Can you see it, nibbling away on those ac**or**ns? How do you think **Or**vil will get past that cow with huge h**or**ns?

fork   horse   sport   storm

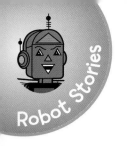

Now three of the five robots in Letterland are broth**er**s: **Er**nest **Er**, Irving Ir and Urgent Ur. They all make the same sound as they report back to Red Robot, but they capture different vowels.

First, let's meet **Er**nest **Er**, the robot who runs away with elephants! When you see **Er**nest **Er** in a word, don't expect to hear Eddy Elephant making his usual sound. All you can hear is **Er**nest **Er** calling out his last name, '**Er**!' as he reports back to Red Robot.

Ernest **Er** is a fast**er** runn**er** than his oth**er** robot broth**er**s. The park rang**er** is c**er**tain he won't be able to catch him as he runs past the beav**er** and the p**er**ch and the ott**er** in the wat**er**. P**er**haps he will al**er**t the helicopt**er** to track down **Er**nest **Er** lat**er**. Right now, the rang**er** had bett**er** look aft**er** the badg**er** and the anteat**er** and the flow**er**s and f**er**ns. What oth**er** animals can you see? And who else can you see working in the park?

danger   flower   panther   tiger

This is **Ir**ving **Ir**. He captures ink, then reports back to Red Robot with his last name, '**Ir**!' so you can't hear Impy Ink making his usual sound. **Ir**ving **Ir** gets into far fewer words than either of his brothers, because most of the ink bottles in Letterland make themselves invisible when they see **Ir**ving **Ir** coming. If Impy Ink gets caught, he squ**ir**ts ink on to **Ir**ving's sh**ir**t! That's why v**ir**tually every sh**ir**t **Ir**ving owns is d**ir**ty!

Irving **Ir** has upset the g**ir**l behind him. She has been planning a th**ir**tieth b**ir**thday party for one of the clowns in the c**ir**cus. She has bought him a new sh**ir**t and cooked him some s**ir**loin steak and a b**ir**thday cake, too! Now the clown with the hose really needs to squ**ir**t the ink off that brand new sh**ir**t! Do you think **Ir**ving **Ir** has seen the acrobats sw**ir**ling around and the g**ir**l tw**ir**ling her baton? Even the c**ir**cus dog is wh**ir**ling round in c**ir**cles.

Can you find th**ir**teen b**ir**ds here at the c**ir**cus today?

bi**rd**   **d**i**rt**   **sh**i**rt**   **sk**i**rt**

This is **Ur**gent **Ur**. You won't see him very often, but when you do, he'll be capturing umbrellas. He reports back to Red Robot with just one word, his last name, '**Ur**!' so you can't hear Uppy Umbrella making her usual sound. **Ur**gent **Ur** must have cold feet, because he always t**ur**ns up wearing boots made of thick c**ur**ly p**ur**ple f**ur**. The boots make him a slower runner than his other brothers, so you hardly ever see him at the end of words.

What an eventful Th**ur**sday in Letterland! Everyone is talking about it! **Ur**gent **Ur** has jumped off the c**ur**b and smashed an **ur**n. He is dist**ur**bing the t**ur**keys, too, though maybe now they'll t**ur**n and see that fox l**ur**king in the bushes. There's a veterinary s**ur**geon's van near the girl who is b**ur**ning leaves. Do you think an animal has been h**ur**t? The cat c**ur**led up by the c**ur**tain doesn't seem to be h**ur**t. Maybe that n**ur**se will be needed to help the man in the h**ur**dle race. He's been h**ur**led right off his horse!

curtain   fur   nurse   purple

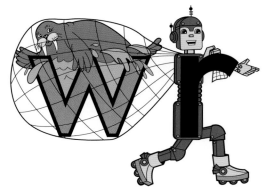

I expect you know that both Walter Walrus and Red Robot are troublemakers in Letterland. So what happens when they meet? Well, Red Robot remembers that Walter causes trouble by splashing water around. But Red Robot doesn't want to get wet. So he quickly captures Walter Walrus in his sack. Then Walter is too shocked to speak! So whenever you see this troublesome pair in a word, expect to hear Red Robot growling, 'rrr...' as he rolls along.

Red Robot has **wr**apped the sack around his **wr**ist so Walter can't **wr**iggle out. "What's **wr**ong with that?" Red Robot says to himself. The little **wr**ens are busy **wr**estling with **wr**iggling worms! Nobody has noticed the **wr**ecking ball knocking down the building behind. What a lot of rubbish in the **wr**eckage! There's some **wr**ought iron, a type**wr**iter, some **wr**apping paper and a poster of a **wr**estling match. **Wr**ite down what you can see in the **wr**eckage.

 **wr**apper    **wr**iggle    **wr**ist    **wr**ong

You may remember that Vowel Men like to go out walking together. When two vowels go out walking, the second one is silent. Do you remember why? He is too busy looking out for vowel-stealing robots. But sometimes, the vowels are not able to spot the robots in time. Then the Vowel Stealers run off with them, changing the sounds they make in words. Carrying two Vowel Men is heavy business. When a robot captures Mr A and Mr I, he always puffs out, '**Air**! I need **air**! I've caught a p**air**!'

There's a lady drying her h**air** downst**air**s in the h**air** salon. She was looking out at the f**air** when she saw a robot sneak up and catch the p**air** of Vowel Men. She was so shocked she dropped her ecl**air** and nearly fell off her ch**air**! It seems so unf**air** of the robot to capture the men at the f**air**. Maybe that little f**air**y can wave her wand and save the p**air**! Have you ever been to a f**air**?

chair   hair   fairy   stair

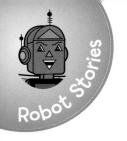

Here again the silent Lookout Man was not able to spot a robot in time, so both Vowel Men are captured. But they don't go quietly! The robot looks away and pretends he can't h**ear** them. He points to his **ear**, still pretending, and says 'Oh d**ear**! I f**ear** my **ear** can't h**ear** you!' Sometimes, you'll also h**ear** him puffing out air again, as they are a heavy pair.

Here we can see the robot capturing the Vowel Men in front of the castle. Noisy Nick is n**ear** the front with his hand to his **ear**. Can you spot Harry Hat Man at the r**ear**? What do you think he will h**ear**? Oh d**ear**! Maybe he will h**ear** those men with b**ear**ds fighting with sp**ear**s. I think they are just practising for a theatre play this y**ear**.

Now that robot is also puffing out air. He will w**ear** himself out! Perhaps he should stop t**ear**ing about and have a juicy p**ear** like those b**ear**s!

oy

There is a b**oy** called R**oy** in Letterland. At the end of words, this b**oy** called R**oy** enj**oy**s leap-frogging over an 'o' and into the Yo-yo Man's sack. He calls this leap-frog game his '**oy** game' because he likes to shout '**oy**!' as he leaps. The Yo-yo Man pretends to be ann**oy**ed so he shouts out '**oy**!' every time R**oy** lands on him unexpectedly.

R**oy** is leap-frogging over an 'o' in a t**oy** shop. There are lots of t**oy**s to enj**oy**, but the queen and that little girl look ann**oy**ed. The queen always looks ann**oy**ed. 'There's too much s**oy** sauce on my **oy**sters! They are destr**oy**ed!' she shouts. I think the girl is ann**oy**ed because she wanted to play with the r**oy**al yacht. Instead she could put on a cowb**oy** hat or pretend she is going on a space v**oy**age. What t**oy** would you like to play with?

annoy   **boy**   **destroy**   **toy**

From time to time, Mr I likes to j**oi**n Roy in playing the 'oy game' but only when they can play it inside words. Why is that? Remember, Mr I always feels dizzy at the end of words. That's when he asks the Yo-yo Man to take over. So now we know why we have two spellings for this one sound – Roy with Mr I inside words and Roy with Yo-yo Man at the end.

Let's j**oi**n Roy and Mr I in this turqu**oi**se kitchen. Mr I is p**oi**nting out of the window at Nick who is making lots of n**oi**se. He was going to go outside and plant more flowers in new s**oi**l, but now he's going to av**oi**d the n**oi**se and finish writing his shopping list.

He's remembered to get f**oi**l and **oi**l, but still needs some t**oi**let rolls, some **oi**ntment and some sirl**oi**n. Now where did he put all of his c**oi**ns?

boil   coin   noise   soil

Mr O has two grandsons. Everyone calls them the 'B**oo**t and Foot Twins' because they spend so much time arguing over their b**oo**ts. When you hear the sound '**oo**' in words like b**oo**t and s**oo**n and z**oo**, you know that the B**oo**t twin is teasing his brother by saying, '**OO**! I have your b**oo**ts!'

The B**oo**t and Foot Twins have come to the z**oo**. There's a sch**oo**l trip today and the children are excited to see the animals. There's a kangar**oo**, a bab**oo**n with a h**oo**p, a cockat**oo**, a m**oo**se, a g**oo**se and a racc**oo**n eating macar**oo**ns, t**oo**! I'm not sure macar**oo**ns are the right kind of f**oo**d for a racc**oo**n, are you?

Can you see another bird by the boy and his ball**oo**n? It's keeping c**oo**l in a little igl**oo**. Have you been to the z**oo**? Which animals would you ch**oo**se to see first?

 b**oo**t   f**oo**d    sp**oo**n   z**oo**

Remember the Boot and F**oo**t Twins are the grandsons of Mr O, the old man. They spend a lot of time arguing over their boots. In most words you will hear the Boot Twin teasing his brother by saying, 'OO! I have your boots!' Sometimes though, you will hear the second twin, the F**oo**t Twin, complaining, '**OO**! Just l**oo**k at my f**oo**t!' as he steps in a puddle.

L**oo**k! The Boot and F**oo**t Twins are in the kitchen. They were planning to c**oo**k some more c**oo**kies from their favourite c**oo**kb**oo**k but the F**oo**t Twin is cross because he has got a wet f**oo**t! That little boy outside is also getting wet as he's left his red coat hanging by the h**oo**d on the h**oo**k. Oh dear! A little dog has come in after playing with a muddy f**oo**tball and now there are f**oo**tprints all over the floor. 'W**oo**f w**oo**f!' he barks - he wants a c**oo**kie, too.

book   cook   foot   wood

There's a giant in Letterland called Giant Full. He helps Mr U put umbrellas in words but sometimes he can be a bit rough. He pushes and pulls the umbrellas. Here's a poor little umbrella that's upside down, saying, 'U! Giant Full, you pushed me in, now pull me out!'

Can you see something else being pushed and pulled? Yes, that bull. Perhaps they are taking him to the field to be with the other bulls. After all that pushing and pulling, they might like to sit on that cushion and have a slice of pudding. There's a full mug of tea and sugar there, too.

Look in the bush! There's a cuckoo. Perhaps that cuckoo would like to eat some pudding. Be careful, little cuckoo. That pussy cat might like to eat you!

bush   bull   cushion   pull

Can you guess whose little brother this is? Yes, it is Oscar's
Bothersome Little Brother. As he is just a baby, he hasn't yet learned
to say 'o' like Oscar. The little brother just says 'uh' in words like love.
He's bothersome because his letter shape looks just like Oscar's.
It's also bothersome that this little brother sounds just like another
Letterlander. He sounds like Uppy Umbrella!

It's Monday in Letterland, and Oscar's Bothersome Little Brother has
come to the park in London. He has a bit of money, so he might buy
some honey. He loves honey. Do you?

On London Road, can you see a mother with her son? I wonder if
they are going on the trip to see the monkeys. There's a poster above
Oscar's little brother about trips to see monkeys every Monday.

It looks like one cheeky monkey has escaped and is somewhere in
London. Can you help discover where he is?

honey money monkey won

Did you also know that Yellow Yo-yo Man loves to appear in words, but sadly there are very few words that need his 'yyy...' sound.

Luckily, Mr I needs his help, too. "Every time I stand at the end of a word," he says, "I feel dizzy! Could you stand at the end of just a few words for me and say my name, **i**?"

Yo-yo Man is happy to help, so now Mr I gives him a free ice cream as a reward – every time!

(e.g. my, try, reply, magnify)

Mr E made so many of his final **e**'s into Silent Magic **e**'s that now he doesn't have enough left for all the words that need his name, **e**, at the end! So he has had to ask Yellow Yo-yo Man to do the job for him. Yellow Yo-yo Man is very happy to help because that gives him a chance to appear at the end of roughly 5,000 words for Mr E!

It's a cold and misty morning in the country. You'd think that Yellow Yo-yo Man would be very chilly, only wearing that shirt, but he is in such a hurry, he hasn't even noticed. He is rushing past a family picnic site where someone has left their teddy. They also left a fairy story book. I hope they find them quickly, before they get frosty.

Yellow Yo-yo Man is going into the city to make twenty copies of a party invitation. He wants plenty of his friends to celebrate with him as he has a new pet puppy. The puppy is tiny, very lively and friendly. He makes Yellow Yo-yo Man happy, and also keeps him very busy. How many of his friends can you see?

why

family   party   puppy   teddy

Vicky Violet's vases ha**ve** a narrow, pointy base, so the slightest breeze can blow them over. The winds in Letterland blow in the Reading Direction, so when the vase is exposed at the end of a word, Vicky puts a silent Vase Prop e right beside the vase to stop it falling over.

This is a very acti**ve** scene with lots going on at the beach. There's a girl sitting on the knee of her relati**ve**. He's given her a gift. She lo**ve**s gifts. Another girl is playing cricket. Look at the ball as it cur**ve**s through the air. Let's hope it doesn't smash into beach hut number twel**ve**, or that table with the oli**ve**s on it.

Ha**ve** you noticed the detecti**ve**? He's searching for clues to sol**ve** a mystery. There has been a break-in at the Letterland castle. Some massi**ve** red jewels have been stolen. Who do you know that might ha**ve** a moti**ve**?

detecti**ve**   lo**ve**   oli**ve**   twel**ve**

  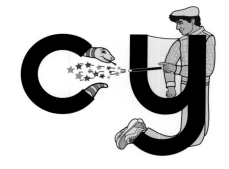

ce ci cy

Clever Cat's secret is she loves to hiss like Sammy Snake, so Mr E invented Blue Magic! When Clever Cat sits next to an **e**, an **i** or a **y**, Blue Magic sparks appear! The sparks are just strong enough to turn Clever Cat into a hissing snake for a little while... ssssss.

Oh look! Clever Cat has turned into a hissing snake right outside the Letterland **ci**ty hospital. It looks like there have been lots of ac**ci**dents in Letterland today. There's an emergen**cy** ambulan**ce** arriving with its lights flashing. There's a little boy who has fallen off his bi**cy**cle, and a man with an i**ce** pack for his sore fa**ce**. He must have been to the pharma**cy** as he also has some medi**ci**ne.

At least those mi**ce** look like they're having a ni**ce** time – dan**ci**ng and balan**ci**ng on that fen**ce**! Careful mi**ce** - no more ac**ci**dents, please!

face mice pencil city cycle

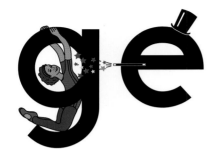  

Golden Girl has a school friend called **Ge**ntle **Ginge**r. Golden Girl is very impressed with **Ge**ntle **Ginge**r's **gy**mnastic skills. She wants everyone to notice, so she asked Mr E to make Blue Magic to light her up. Blue Magic is not powerful, and it doesn't jump over letters. It just lights up **Ge**ntle **Gi**nger so she starts to say her name when she's next to an **e**, **i** or **y**!

Look! Here's **Ge**ntle **Gi**nger at the Letterland **gy**m. She's a member of a **gy**mnastic club. Lots of people go to the **gy**m. The girl with the frin**ge** likes yoga. She's had an ener**gy** drink to keep herself going. The boy by the **gi**raffe poster looks full of ener**gy**. Perhaps he's had an oran**ge**, a tan**ge**rine, a ve**ge**table smoothie or an ener**gy ge**l! He's probably about to do some more **gy**mnastics. Can you do any **gy**mnastics?

orange   page   giraffe   energy

Kicking King loves kicking but Noisy Nick has a **kn**ack of getting in his way. Instead of kicking and making his sound he frowns and stays silent.

Kicking King and Noisy Nick are visiting friends. Noisy Nick likes this house as there are toy **kn**ights to play with. The girl **kn**eeling down is playing with the **kn**ights and there are two more friends **kn**ocking at the door.

Kicking King has no room to kick so he **kn**ows he has to stay silent. Instead he just watches the lady **kn**itting. Her **kn**itting may well get in **kn**ots because a kitten is playing with the wool. Oh no! I can see a **kn**ot already! Can you?

knee   **k**night   **k**nife   **k**not

Clever Cat says 'c' in words and Harry Hat Man says 'h'. When they sit together his hairy hat tickles her nose and she sneezes 'ch!'

Occasionally though, Harry's hat blows off in the wind. Clever Cat doesn't sneeze. She says 'c' again and Harry is too startled to speak!

Look! A gust of wind has blown Harry's hat off in school! So all we can hear is Clever Cat's little 'c' sound in the word school. She likes school because she can learn a lot and become even more clever. I think she is learning about chemistry today. There are some chemicals and books about chemistry on the table, by the orchid. What time of year do you think it is in Letterland? Ah yes, there's a clue. The school choir and the orchestra are advertising their Christmas concerts. Harry Hat Man's hat blows off in choir as well!

school   choir   mechanic   orchestra

← School Archive

Technology in Chemistry

Choir
Choral Chords at Christmas

School Orchestra
Christmas Concert

Architect

Aches
Headache
Stomach ache

Understanding the Chemistry

Chemical

Chlorine

Echoes
Chemistry

Christine Nichols

Mr Mean-E is a grumpy old man who likes to make spelling difficult. He tries to trick us by looking like an **e** but sounding like an **a**. He is too mean to be seen very often in words, but you can see him in the word 'th**ey**'.

Today, Mr Mean-E is out walking in words, trying to trick us. He's been doing it all his life, and he's now **e**ighty **e**ight!
The sky is gr**ey** and it has snowed. A r**e**indeer is pulling a sl**e**igh in the snow. Can you see the horse? Perhaps it n**e**ighed when it saw the ospr**ey** catch its pr**ey**. Or perhaps the noise of the fr**e**ight train, or that girl suddenly abs**e**iling down the gr**ey** cliff surprised the horse. That man in b**e**ige is shouting at his dog. But his dog is disob**ey**ing him. "H**ey**! Get out of the way of Mr Mean-E!"

eight   sl**e**igh   pr**ey**   gr**ey**

In Letterland there is a teacher called Mr '**Tion**. One day, he had a tea party for his class, but first they had to do a spelling quiz. He asked, "Can anyone spell my name?" Many children tried to spell it the way it sounds, with 'sh'. But that was wrong. Finally Nick, who was thirsty for tea, managed to spell it correctly. Mr '**Tion** smiled and gave everyone a trick way to remember how to spell his name when he said: "Here's the **T**ea **I O**we **N**ick." Remembering Mr '**Tion**'s trick will help you spell it correctly, too!

We are back in the Letterland school today with the teacher Mr '**Tion**. He's teaching addi**tion**, subtrac**tion**, multiplica**tion** and frac**tion**s. There's so much to learn and lots of new words to look up in the dic**tion**ary. The children will all need a lot of concentra**tion** to understand frac**tion**s. How will they concentrate with all the construc**tion** noise outside?

addition   **dictionary**   **caution**   **portion**

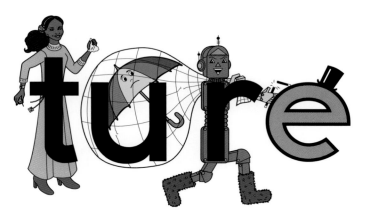

As Urgent Ur runs past Talking Tess, he hears her sneeze, just like Clever Cat does sometimes, 'ch'. Urgent Ur always overpowers the Magic **e** at the end to make sure it can't turn his stolen umbrella into a Vowel Man. When you see these letters, you'll hear this sound, '**ture**'.

Look in this pic**ture** at the mix**ture** of things going on. There's an adven**ture** park and some cows in a pa**sture**. That strange crea**ture** on the bench is a vul**ture**. There's a man making a sculp**ture** of the vul**ture**. I wonder if he came to the park on his bike? He'll be sad when he sees that his bike has a punc**ture**. Another woman is painting a pic**ture** of a little girl on her bike. It looks good. When she's finished, she'll add her signa**ture**. Can you hear Talking Tess sneezing in words in this pic**ture**?

 furniture  nature  sculpture  vulture

all

Giant All is a really lazy old giant. If he can find another word to lean on while he eats an apple, he will. He likes leaning far more than standing on his own two feet. You can only see one of his legs when he is leaning because one is behind the other.

This is Giant **All,** and he is so t**all** that you can't even see the top of him. **All** we can see are his long legs. He seems to be grabbing an apple. Giant **All** loves apples. In fact, he loves them so much that he just strides into words and takes them without asking! So if you spot a word with an apple in it, but to the right of that apple there are the two long legs of Giant **All,** don't expect to hear that apple saying its usual sound. Instead, **all** you will hear is Giant **All,** c**all**ing his own name '**All**'.

Giant **All** is not the only one c**all**ing out today. There's also a boy by the water**fall** c**all**ing his dog, but his dog is busy chasing a b**all**. Maybe the dog found the b**all** at that st**all** or in the hold**all**. Can you spot another sm**all** boy in the picture? I hope he is jumping and not f**all**ing from that climbing frame! It's lots of fun to climb trees, climbing frames and balance on w**all**s but we **all** need to be careful not to f**all**.

almost

ball

call

tall

waterfall

Ball stall

3 for 2
small balls

all

ful

Giant Full is a lazy old giant. He tries to help Mr U collect umbrellas. He pushes and pulls them into u's until they are full. But he's very lazy, so he often pulls up a word next to him to lean on. When he leans on a word, be care**ful**, as you will only see one of his legs!

It's another beauti**ful** day in Letterland. Giant Full has been admiring the wonder**ful** things at the market. A man tried to sell him a hand**ful** of beans and a lady came with an arm**ful** of jeans for him to try on. Finding jeans for such long legs can be awfully tricky, but she was very help**ful**.

Giant Full has a cup**ful** of tea and a plate**ful** of delight**ful** pancakes. He's now leaning back relaxing again. That position looks pain**ful**, but he says it's rest**ful**!

handful **mouthful** **playful** **spoonful**

When a Magic **e** is next to Lucy Lamp Light sometimes the magic sparks change Lucy into a large magical cand**le**! When the cand**le** is burning it can send magic sparks up and over one letter.

map becomes **maple**   **cab** becomes **cable**

This Cand**le** Magic is not strong enough to send magic over more than one letter. So here's a spelling trick, if you don't want Cand**le** Magic to make a vowel man appear, add a Best Friend to protect the vowel.

pad becomes **paddle**

There is Cand**le** Magic outside the stab**le**, under the map**le** tree. It looks like someone had a picnic with nood**le**s, app**le**s and jelly that wobb**le**s. I wonder why they did not use the tab**le**? Maybe it was too close to the pudd**le**s. Or maybe it was just nicer to sit under the map**le** and play with the marb**le**s and puzz**le** pieces.

table   title   puzzle   apple

STABLES

The Little Book
of Fables

Do you remember, when Noisy Nick and Golden Girl sit together, they are so happy they sing!

Now, Magic -**ing** was made by accident! Just after Mr E invented his Magic **e**'s he took his hat off and and rested it on an -**ing** end**ing**. His hat was still full of magic because the -**ing** end**ing** became magical, too. Mr E decided it was quite excit**ing** to have -**ing** as a magic end**ing**.

Can you see all the fascinat**ing** things go**ing** on in Letterland today? There are children rac**ing** each other, a girl rid**ing** a bike and a boy rid**ing** a horse. Another boy has been bak**ing**. I think the girl roller-skat**ing** might like to try his bak**ing**. Even the man parachut**ing** is looking at his bak**ing**!

 driving

 racing

 skating

 smoking

Word List

ar
archery board
alarm
armadillo
bark
barn
car
cart
carve/carving
chart
dark
dart
farmer
farmyard
garden
guitar
market
postcards
radar
scarlet
scarf
star
tart
varnish

or
acorn
corn
corner
fork
horns
horse
morning
north

orchard
orchids
porcupine
sports
score
shore
stork
storm
shorts
tornado

er
anteater
badger
beaver
butterfly
carpenter
cleaner
danger
fern
flowers
hammer
helicopter
herbs
ladder
otter
painter
panther
perch
pliers
ranger
spider
tiger
timber

water
water lily
woodpecker

ir
birch
birds
birthday cake
circus
dirty
girder
girl
headfirst
fir cones
ladybird
shirt
sirloin steak
skirt
squirt
swirl
twirl

ur
burger
burn
burrs
conjurer
curb
curl
curtain
disturb
frankfurters
fur
furniture

hurdles
lurk
nurse
Saturday
surgery
Thursday
turkey
turnip
urn
windsurf

wr
typewriter
wrapping
wreath
wreck
wren
wrench
wrestling
wriggle
wrinkles
wring
wristwatch
writhe
writing paper
wrong
wrought iron

air
air
chair
Claire
dairy
eclair

fair
hair
hairspray
hairdryer
pair of scissors
stairs

ear or ear/air/*
appear
beard
clear
ear
dear
fear
gear
hear
near
rear
spear
tear
year
bear*
pear*
tear*
swear*
wear*

oy
annoyed
boy
corduroy
cowboy hat
destroy
gargoyle

royal
soy
toy
voyage

oi
boil
boiler
coil
coins
foil
noise
oil
ointment
point
poison
Polaroid
sirloin
soil
toilet roll
tortoise

oo
baboon
bamboo
balloon
boot
broom
cockatoo
food
goose
hoop
igloo
kangaroo

62

macaroon
moon
moose
racoon
school
spoon
stool
tools
zoo

oo
book
childhood
foot
cookbook
cookies
cooker
football
hood
hook
wood
woof
wool

u
bull
butcher
bush
cuckoo
cushion
full
pudding
pull
push

pussy cat
sugar

o
come
company
dove
honey
gloves
London
Monday
money
monkey
month
mother
son
won

y
berry
Bouncy Ben
bunny
Dippy Duck
dummy
fairy
family
frosty
holly
ivy
misty
party
puppy
story
teddy

Vicky Violet

ve
curve
detective
exclusive
love
motive
olives
olive oil
relative
twelve

ce
ambulance
balance (mice)
centre
dance
December
entrance
face
fence
finance
ice pack
mice
office(s)
science
service
space

ci
accident
circle
cirrus clouds

city
medicine
pencil

cy
bicycle
cyclist
cylinder
emergency
pharmacy
recycle

ge
danger (sign)
fringe (girl)
gel
germs
gentlemen
Manager's Office
orange
tangerine
vegetables

gi
ginger
giraffe
hygiene gel
magic wand

gy
energy drink
energy gel
gym
gymnast

gymnastics club

kn
knapsack
knee
kneel
knickers
knife
knights
knitting needle
knitting
knob
knock
knocker
knot
knowledge
knuckle

ch
ache
anchor (t-shirt)
architect
archive
characters
chemist
chemistry
chlorine
choir
choral
chords
Christine Nichols
Christmas
chrome

echoes
headache
mechanic
orchid
orchestra
stomach
technology

e
abseil
beige
grey
disobey
eight
freight
hey
neigh
obey
osprey
prey
reins
reindeer
survey
weight

-tion
action
addition
caution
construction
correction
dictionary
exhibition

exploration
fiction
fraction
introduction
multiplication
portion
section
subtraction

-ture
adventure
architecture
creature
culture
departure
furniture
future

gesture (wave)
literature
mixture
nature
pasture
picture
portraiture
puncture (bike)
sculpture
signature
vulture

all
ball
call
fall
holdall

small
stall
tall
wall
waterfall

-ful
armful
basketful
bowlful
bucketful
colourful
cupful
handful
mouthful
painful
plateful
playful

restful
spoonful

-le
apple
beetle
bottle
bridle
castle
drizzle
eagle
fables
giggle (children)
huddle (children)
hurdle
kettle
little (children)
marbles

maple
noodles
puzzle
puddle
wobble (jelly)
stable
table
thistle

-ing
baking
driving
exciting
fading (light)
gliding (birds)
parachuting
racing
riding (bike)

riding (horse)
roller-skating
shining
slicing
smiling
smoking

Published by Letterland International Ltd
Leatherhead, Surrey, KT22 9AD, UK

LETTERLAND® is a registered trade mark of Lyn Wendon.

British Library Cataloguing in Publication Data. A catalogue record for this book is available from the British Library.

Written by Lisa Holt & Lyn Wendon, originator of Letterland
Original illustrations by Doreen Shaw, Geri Livingston & Lisa Holt
Adapted by Isabelle Nicolle & Laura Bittles
Design by Lisa Holt

Printed in China